Thomas Robinson Hazard, J. T. Staats

Inspirational Writings of Mrs. J. T. Staats

Thomas Robinson Hazard, J. T. Staats

Inspirational Writings of Mrs. J. T. Staats

ISBN/EAN: 9783337182137

Printed in Europe, USA, Canada, Australia, Japan

Cover: Foto ©ninafisch / pixelio.de

More available books at **www.hansebooks.com**

SPIRITUAL COMMUNION, TRACT No. 6.

INSPIRATIONAL WRITINGS

OF

MRS. J. T. STAATS,

OF NEW YORK,

WRITTEN IN THE PRESENCE OF THE COMPILER,

THOMAS R. HAZARD.

BOSTON:
COLBY & RICH,
No. 9 MONTGOMERY PLACE.
1876.

INTRODUCTION.

Mrs. J. T. STAATS, the inspired writer of the following spiritual communications, was one of the first, as also one of the best, of the prophets or mediums who have been used as instruments by the angelic world in working the great revolution in thought and religious belief and knowledge that has pervaded the civilized world during the last twenty-seven years. Mrs. Staats is a lady of culture and social position, and it is to be regretted that she cannot be prevailed upon to furnish for publication a detailed narrative of the early and progressive steps that led to the exercise of the beautiful and beneficent gift of spiritual mediumship which she has so faithfully devoted herself to for about twenty years.

In a letter to the compiler of the communications, under date of Oct. 13th, 1875, Mrs. Staats writes:

"I thank you for the kindness shown me, and assure you that it would afford me pleasure to give some satisfactory account of what you are pleased to term my 'extraordinary gift.' Unfortunately I have no date at which *this* now called 'mediumship' began with me, from my earliest recollection my childhood days having been made happy in the enjoyment of the society of playmates and companions who were invisible to others, though real and beautiful to me. Education strove to convince me that it was wrong to encourage my *dreaming* and *seeming* fancies. But both human reasoning and the constructions placed upon the *sacred word* by learned men, failed to prove to me that the *devil* was answering the demands of my affections when they so earnestly pleaded within me for a satisfactory answer to the momentous question, 'If a loved one die shall he live again?'

"Observation taught and drew me nearer to God through the works of Nature, whose grand and simple lessons I revered from the fact that they never lead astray. My intuitions brought to my knowledge authority so far above my limited material senses, and so unfolded the functions of my spirit, that I ceased to *fear*, *doubt* or question my right and privilege to go direct to the fountain of light and receive from thence that which the great Spirit Father giveth unto all that sincerely ask, viz., 'every good and perfect gift.'

"It may not become me to say how perfect *my gift* is, further than that to me it is *good*, and I only regret that the pressure of constantly recurring family duties has not permitted me to devote more time to it than I have been able to.

"Much as you have said in defence of mediums, still more remains to be said of a class who are without parallel almost wholly misunderstood, and hence almost wholly *misjudged;* beings who are keenly sensitive from the nature of their gift; sought for in seasons of bereavement and sorrow to lift the shadows and burdens from the hearts of afflicted ones whose strength and resources are far greater than their own, but who, when the clouds have departed, are seldom called upon to share the joys of those they have been made the instruments in the hands of the angels to relieve. Alas! I wonder that so many remain true and faithful to their high calling."

The communications in this number (six) have all been given within the last three or four years. They are arranged without regard to dates, as they were not preserved with a view of being printed, especially as many of them are of a personal and domestic character. They are given to the public, however, for a purpose, in connection with the five numbers of the series of tracts that precede them in order of number, the compiler believing that but few who have the inclination or patience to peruse the six little volumes carefully will fail to observe how closely the identity of each communicating spirit is preserved throughout, although speaking through many different mediums of widely varying character, education and culture, and residing in some instances hundreds of miles apart, and entirely unacquainted with each other. In every instance, though the language may be that of the medium, it may be observed that the ideas and sentiments expressed through the one are always congenial with those expressed through the organisms of the other instruments of the communicating spirits. T. R. H.

Vaucluse, Rhode Island, January, 1876.

INSPIRATIONAL MESSAGES

THROUGH THE MEDIUMSHIP OF

MRS. J. STAATS.

MY DEAR HUSBAND—We meet you this morning with our usual strength, and make here for you a new point of communication. Not that we can say anything new, but that it is pleasant to greet you whenever I can offer another expression of love and kindness, and now that you require only the affectional, I saw in this medium, as we mentally controlled, an entire absence of the test magnetism. Hence I have said I cannot tell you anything new.

Anna is with me, and we will do all that is possible for us to do to add another and a sweeter link in the chain of evidences which draws your spirit nearer to the skies. Now, my dear one, this sitting will be productive of nothing that to your ears will be new, but then as expressions of love are never wearying, and always sweetly welcome, I shall express, and continue to express my love, so that you will be happier if not wiser. I find all things connected with home in a very harmonious state. The girls are happy in that fullness of faith which discloses to them our presence, and makes them to feel that the chain is not broken but growing each day stronger and brighter. Anna felt a little disappointed at first that her cousin did not come again to this medium. Oh how strange that another's unbelief should fall like a stone heavy and damp, crushing out the sweet flowers which affection and truth implant in the heart. I am glad that the ridicule which others use so freely does not disturb you: I anxiously trust it never may. I want you to stand as you ever have in the affectional and natural, reaching but a little way, for you know how easy it is for me to clasp your hand. Anna feels quite sure that she can give her picture through the spirit artist Anderson. You might try it if you like, and yet I can see that your own mind will have to watch a certain condition to harmonize with ours before you can succeed. FANNY.

DEAR FATHER AND BROTHER—We are with you to-night, in full possession of our spiritual bodies, and there is so much we wish to say to you that we scarce know where to begin or what to tell. Of our home we will not attempt a description, for you know our influences, and have as perfect a knowledge of it as we are able to give you. Our lives are blended with yours, and we are happy in the progress you are making. The truth is that the spiritual outpouring is beginning to be felt everywhere, and all the promises which the angels made when you, dear father, first began to investigate, are everywhere apparent. Go, by all means, to Moravia, where we can gather and give to you the best of all evidences. We will come to you, telling you that we retain all our faculties, and are happiest when we can bless you. Take our united blessing and love, and feel, dear father and brother, that you have the constant guidance of your loving band with ANNA.

Thee knows, my son, that it is an easy thing for men to promise, and quite as easy for a spirit. I promise thee to be with thy circle at Moravia. Thy wife and children may not appear in the first sitting, but thee must make up thy mind to remain and be patient, for much will be given thee. With much love from thy father and mother, GRANDFATHER HAZARD.

December 21st, 1871.

MY DEAR HUSBAND—I am very glad to meet you here again. I have felt that you needed another sitting with me before you made up your mind to go to Moravia. I can help you to some very direct and positive tests by going and staying long enough. I was up there with some friends, and saw the *modus operandi*, and think that nothing will be required but to wait patiently, giving us plenty of opportunity, so that you can take away with you all that you need to finish your faith. Anna is particularly desirous, and indeed so are all the circle. Several have promised to join you, and I assure you that we feel a great interest in the trial.

I am particularly well pleased with B.'s position and progress, and I know that you can see the effects of our influence all about him. Dear boy! he has a beautiful life before him, and is certainly in the right place.

I am not going to promise too much, but say to you that I know we can come to you at Moravia, and that you will recognize me. I shall help you to be in the right condition, and I feel that you are fully prepared for all that is being prepared to meet you. Oh, how beautiful the thought, and how happy is the circle which surrounds you here to-day. There are many who come through the welcome which the spirit extends to you. I shall help you to move on in the path of life, coming at last when I can open the door into our beautiful and eternal home. With abundance of love to all our dear ones, I am your spirit-wife, FANNY.

You see, my dear one, that I do not dictate to you in anything. I am satisfied with your happiness, and if all are content and harmonious in

the faith and light which makes us still one
individual family, gathering from the beautiful
gardens flowers of truth which all may enjoy,
and still journey on together until we meet in
this our delightful spiritual home. Anna has
taken a seat at your side, and with others awaits
their turn to express as I have words of truth
and love. Why, my dear one, the room is full of
spirits, not only our kindred but sweet and loving spirits whose circles we enjoy, as you will
when you enter the beautiful gate left ajar for
you. Oh how joyous! I cannot bear to leave,
but Anna must add her chaplet of fresh roses.

FANNY.

Yes, dear father, here we are, and so happy.
I wish you could hear my song this morning, and
feel my love, all that I have to bring; but you
could not endure it all. Oh, dear father, it is
impossible for me to tell you what I see and how
much enjoyment, surprise and delight, succeed
each other at every point. I am so glad to be
able to direct my magnetism upon you. I gain
strength very rapidly, and I was most happy
when I found myself possessing the power to
move about my home with my new or spiritual
powers of locomotion. I want you to tell G——
that I am enabled to bring a new spirit to her,
one who is going to make her write some very
sweet and beautiful inspirations. She ought to
take a great deal of out-door exercise, and I will
be with her to write in the morning, the first and
best hour of all the day, when the body is refreshed and there is no over-action of the stomach to draw upon the brain. I see many of those
who were in the habit of communicating to us,
and through them I have been attracted to others
still higher and more fully developed. Why, do
you know, father, that your father and mother
look young and beautiful? and many come here
to the spirit-land with their errors so firmly fixed
that they do not recognize their nearest friends.
I have often been amused to see them; and again

it develops my charity to find that so much that is beautiful and every way useful should be shut out from the soul. My dear father, we can and do protect you from danger, and impart to you at the right time all that you need for any purpose and development, for we do talk face to face with you.

There are so many in the room that I shall be obliged to let the sweet and beautiful little Indian girl which I see here talk for them. Auntie, mother dear, and myself, are a strong trio, and we join in abundance of love to the dear ones all, but most especially to those who welcome us. Love to Aunt A. also, and to all who welcome me. There, dear father, I will let them talk now. Always your loving spirit daughter, with my spirit mother.
    ANNA P., with LUCY and MARY.

———

My son, there is more of this truth abroad in the world than you are aware of yet, and the time is not distant when all the great plans of the angels will be shown, and you will be most thankful for the things you have suffered. I say to you fear not, but believe as ever in the ministry of angels. GRANDFATHER HAZARD.

———

DEAR FATHER—We bless you to-night, and have come to make you feel that you are not alone, although so many loved ones have gone from your external sight. The veil is so thin to-night that we look from behind its folds and show you the light of a brighter hope and a more perfect immortality. Do not think we have been unmindful of your needs. My dear father, there are many roses yet to bloom for you, and you will know our love through all. Bless our dear brother, and believe us always in love your own happy circle. Uncle and grandfather are here with you to answer much that you

desire to know. Always your own loving Anna
—with all the buds ripened here.*

MY DEAR FATHER—We come this morning, as we knew that you were to be here. We found no difficulty in controlling the hand of the medium. We talk face to face with you, and can impress you wherever you are. Yet you are not at all times cognizant of what we would wish to tell you. As we remain longer in the spirit-life we learn more and more of the connections which bind spirit to spirit. We see you as our natural father, and the ties of consanguinity which hold us to you make us to revolve in one sphere of thought, your spirit progressing in equal ratio with my own. Many times when your body is sleeping we come and take your spirit, and it leaves the material as readily almost as in death. And while at times there are visions foreshadowded from the spirit to the outer senses they are those things which cannot be expressed. I am happy in the employment which my spirit finds in music, poetry, and all that I longed to learn in life. And yet even that does not render me so entirely happy as to come and talk with you, through thoughts of the future. I shall see Aunt Gertrude, and send her if you would like, now. Good-by. I know she will want to see you about her sister. I am still your ever loving daughter, ANNA.

You are going down home, are you not? I almost wish I could go with you in the old way, and take one more look, and hear all my loved ones congratulate me upon my improved health and strength. And your brother would want to inquire after my sister Fanny, and try to find out if she and I were together. I want to talk of the last one that came to spirit-life, and of the

* Three immature births.

one that is soon to follow her, but do n't you tell her that I said so. The last one that came here is present, and wants to speak to you before you go up to see her loved ones. GERTRUDE.

Tell my loved ones to lay aside all sorrow, for that is not a grief that makes my spirit glad. Tell them that none that love those gone before should mourn longer than nature within them or habit requires.

I know that they experience the lonely and sinking feeling of the heart that every child must feel after the loved form of their mother has been laid away from their sight. But the aching loving life that actuated that body still hovers near them, and would bid them call it no more till it has had its sweet and peaceful rest that after suffering must come. I shall not speak to my son yet. I know that his spirit will bid me rest as soon as his own can do so. I shall be with them soon again to bid them harmonize their spirits together, that they may again be reünited to me when time shall be with them no more. And now ask me questions, that I may send them some further assurance of my individuality. How is my sick sister? I only hope that they will ask you, and then you can give them this. I know that D. would not listen, but I hope my sister A. would. He dislikes to think of death, and this reminds him of it. He puts it out of his mind altogether, but their thinking of me brings me back here, and I often wish they would not dwell upon it so much. CAROLINE.

I have not been here long. There are others here, and I think they can tell you more than they have as yet. You know that when the mind first has a new idea presented to its view it takes a stronger hold of every mental feeling than it does after it has become accustomed to it.

Therefore a spirit that has been here but a few weeks or months is much better prepared to tell you of this home and life, and to compare those with the last scenes on earth *than one that has been here as long as I have.* We have all had a blessed visit with you at this time, a much sweeter one than you can often let us have, and as your mind becomes more and more influenced by our own we can all the better feel that your spirit lived with our own and that your body only stayed to protect those we love. And now, dear loved one, I go, and Mary will speak next. I too shall see you again, and often, but I do not know exactly when I can communicate again—but I take each and every opportunity that offers itself, and rejoice none the less if there are hours and not days that fall between.

Yours ever, FANNY.

I love to be there with you all, and I love to keep with you when I can, and I would that I could tell them all of my studies as they come up before me in all their attractive loveliness of new and harmonious ideas. I think that sister G. understands me best. I will tell you what I have learned in my studies of harmonious attractions between particles that have an affinity to one another. I am taught to always learn to group in texture, and not in color or outward appearance. And it is just so with the mind as it is with colors, some absorb and retain, some deflect rather than absorb, and this makes the seeming difference, and all things in nature are but the alphabet of the more growing mind of man, and from man germinates an individual spirit, and this spirit must be assigned its position through a knowledge not of its seeming attractions but from its texture or reasoning understanding. This I am taught to believe will yet be the religion of earth—but the time has not yet come to harmonize the judges that are to assign the grouping. My sister F. is not as near me as my sister G. is, for she cannot understand things that do not appeal to her outward feelings, and yet sister G. is the sensitive impulsive spirit whose spirit will often be led to sorrow on account of too much sensibility and of having people to misunderstand her, more than sister F. will. They are not yet matured—the germ is not yet filled. I have the little ones with me. MARY.

DEAR FATHER—Aunt Agatha, mother and myself, with the dear home circle, are about you, and as ever glad to send welcome to your spirit. I know that you will be well repaid for going where a greater force can be brought to greet you. I am watching ——, and I am greatly encouraged with all that I see for her. If the changes which have passed in her can be made plain to her external senses she can be made to make her experiences very useful. I see her gentle yet nervous—highly so; all remains now upon the locality and what she has about her. This we will quietly help her to select. Dear mother and myself have special care of her, but we have to move with great caution to keep out all cross currents. I see no reason why there should be a return; there need not if all things are kept in order, and we shall help her to make her own selections. You, dear father, and the dear ones have suffered more than she has. We feel that her life has been spared for a good purpose, and I know that her future will be one of great importance, provided we can express through her what we wish to. You will have to be cautious with my sisters relative to their care of her. I know that all of you will be blessed with her love. I am so glad to see dear brother so happy. I know that he is in the right place. We watch over him with love. ANNA.

MY DEAR ONE—Anna, as you see, was the first to talk to you. Aside from the happiness which we enjoy in this pleasant communion, we are delighted with the interest manifested by those whom your faith has reached away out in the realms of darkness.* They saw you as one of the very few who was ready to be the patient helper of the spirits in darkness. We have now a complete circle, in which there are all kinds and conditions of life. We hope you will continue in them, for you will help the world to send missionaries afar into the spirit-life. I see all our loved ones, and I know that you will do your work with our help, working out in harmony all the uses of life and yet being in life immortal with your faithful spirit-wife. FANNY.

---

* * * I have tried to manifest to my sisters, and they have seen and felt us. I can only repeat this again and again, and I know that you will be happy with us throughout eternity. Do not, my dear father, think that sister F.'s opposition comes from disrespect for you; it is only the result of education, and she will not change so long as she stands upon that basis, which she holds through materiality alone. Her spirit accepts, but the letter exerts its power, and she lives in it and will in all probability remain there while she is in earth-life. She does not grieve us. Mother and myself can guard and protect her, and come with the same love to bless her on the way of life and truth with peace and happiness. I cannot tell you anything new. Now as I look about you, I see so many of the old circle gathering, that I must relinquish the pencil to them and let each say a word. I am sure of your spirit being with ours, and you will know me as ever thy lily of the life immortal.

In love, your daughter ANNA.

We greet thee, friend, and I am glad to assure thee that no thought is lost. If thy thoughts

---

*Referring to some of the characters given in the "ORDEAL OF LIFE."

connected with this man of earthly power were expressed, they were immortal. And thy greater faith enabled us to bring thee many strong and faithful spirits. I know that the things expressed by this man Hughes are truth, and I was one of the first to take him by the hand and lead him into the simple walks of godliness. He had a good heart and a broad nature; hence was capable of laying aside the bonds which held him to his forms. He is an active working spirit in this great cause. I am ready to assure thee that his ideas, though harmonizing with thine as expressed by the medium, are not necessarily influenced by thy mind.* A great crowd of influences are pressing upon thee, and they impress thoughts on thy mind, leading thee but little, it is true, but always in harmony with thee. Thy friend,

WILLIAM PENN.

MY DEAR HUSBAND—We come to you this morning full of hope and love, all much happier now that we have accomplished so much for your faith and hope, to say that we are not interested in all you do. You know it would be impossible. Hence we let that which you know, form a basis for all your future, knowing that there are joys which we cannot appreciate, save in the full acceptance of our own interior intercourse with one another. I can speak plainer to your spirit through the medium of your own thoughts than I can through the hand or lips of a stranger. What I say to you, then, comes direct from me, and your answer or acceptance of what I give is just as satisfactory to me as to see you accepting it through the hand of a medium. That you do more good to others by sitting with mediums, I have no doubt, and I am happy to greet you at all places when I can; but then I am happier in

---

*I had just been communing with a spirit purporting to be Bishop Hughes, whose ideas seemed in such harmony with my own that I suspected them to be a reflex of my own mind.

your own thoughts. I see you at places where
other spirits press close to you, anxious to give
you words of truth, and then and there of course
I remain silent at your side while they speak to
you. Then again, when they cannot gain control, and strive to do so, I always aid them, and
bring a kindly influence to assist them in their
work. I shall help you ever and always to make
more perfect the harmony between us all, and as
I gain strength to go to others, I also bring a
power to act upon the children, each according
as they are capable of attracting.

You wonder, no doubt, how it was that G. had
a relapse. We did all we could to prevent her
going to work in the house, but as we had to do
all we did through you, the opposition which
you must then have brought would have been
quite as detrimental as the excitement which
followed. Hence we can only say that her own
experience, after all, will probably be better
for her. She has so much ambition it is the most
difficult matter to make her see that she is unable
to go through with what she undertakes. If I
can impress her to remain quiet at such times
when rest is the only remedy, I shall be glad,
and I do hope to overcome entirely all such conditions in the future.

I shall help you to further pleasant investigation. I know that in all this truth there is
still much more to be learned, and he who
seeks it in the right spirit will surely gain a
reward worthy his faith. Be strong, and as
ever your own best judge of truth. Our dear
ones are learning through the experiences of the
earth-life, problems, and bringing wisdom and
love to illuminate the darkness. B. is all that we
could wish, and we have a care constantly over
him. All the rest have our care, and we will aid
them to protect and individualize themselves, so
that the strange incongruities of life will not af-
fect or disturb their progress. Do not feel in
haste about going home. You had better be sure
that there is no danger of F.'s taking cold before you leave the city, as the measles are certain

to fall on the lungs provided they do not fully work out through the surface. All that is needed is quiet and warmth to keep the disease on the surface. I shall be with you and all the circle as ever, watchful and unwearied in love.

  Your own   FANNY, *with the children.*

MY DEAR ONE—I do not say that B. will have the measles, but I think from the state I see him in, he is far more likely to do so than E. He is weary at night and sympathetic when he comes home, and in that state has not the positive power to resist. I will spread our magnetic influence about him in such a way that he will feel my protection, and keep him from it just as far as possible. He has worked his way on thus far so nobly, so bravely, that I am anxious he should have no drawback. Keep him out of F.'s room when she is getting better, and let her see him only outside of the magnetism of her own chamber. It is when it is being thrown off that the disease most affects others. We are all ready to assist just as far as our own powers will enable us to, and we know that you will be each day more and more cognizant of the individual presence which we bring. G. is very quiet at this time, and feeling very well. Do not be uneasy in regard to her. We will divide the circle and watch in both places, when we can see our presence needed. In love and truth, ever your own loving spirit-wife,   FANNY M. H.'

I said jocosely, "I suppose Anna will be offended if I do n't ask for her?"

Oh no, dear father, I am not going to be offended, and have no such thought. And then I have so much to attend to! I want to be with you, then too with G., and again with F. and E. You know that dear mother and I are ever active, each attending to our duties, and that we love to go where but few others reach. I look forward to some beautiful seasons at home this summer, when all of us are gathered there, and we shall then make you to feel more than ever happy with your circle of loved ones and your own ANNA.

MY FRIEND—You propound to me an important question, which is but little understood by Spiritualists generally, in regard to individual spirit control. My answer is: I can control media in different directions, and yet not always be able to tell to one what I had communicated through another. We withdraw and place our power to suit the occasion, or if I may so say, the demand, which we see, regardless of the proof of identity, on which you place so much importance. We saw that you were the right person to go to Moravia, and selected you accordingly to do what was done there, which in the end will result in great good to the cause. Hence it made no difference whether I proved my identity to you in the way you expected so long as I did all that you wished, and still something more that the circle wanted done, to further their great purpose with humanity through your interviews with those at Moravia, and your help to other mediums you met there, who are perhaps as good, if properly developed, as those who are dwelling there. I want you to know that we can scatter the seeds of spiritual truths through your mind, for the good reason of your broad faith, and the truth that we have helped to brighten shall through your instrumentality brighten others.

I come to you in your hours of writing and express myself through you quite readily, and am happy in doing so from the fact that I can give out to the world facts which are incontrovertible. I am aware of the growing interest which exists everywhere, and I am delighted with every prompt answer that is conveyed to humanity through an unquestionable source. Not that I would reject truth anywhere or from

any source, but because I know how determinedly a large majority resist the truth when they find an opportunity to find fault with the instrument which conveys it. You will be at work. I shall go with you, and you will not regret the presence of your friends, nor will you weary in the labor they ask of you with your friend
THEODORE PARKER.

My Dear One—You know we always come first in the circle when we greet you. With our influence about you, then all the other friends can come in and offer the evidences of their love and care. I know that you feel satisfied whether we do or do not succeed in giving them all that you wish to hear from them. Grandfather is here, and always regrets that he is not entirely able to give you the full and perfect accounts that you require to do well with. I want him to impress you directly in your business, but I find that the question of time does disturb him, and he cannot calculate when the result will come. Then as you well know there are so many changes every day occurring, that even if seen in the mind of man to do, it does not always follow that it will be possible for the man to accomplish what he had previously fully determined to do. Therefore you cannot say that they are unreliable. I want you to be quiet, and not make many movements in the business world until you know just what to do, for the time has come when you will work with us, and help so entirely to do our work that you will not require another party. I am with you in so much that is thought that I cannot ofttimes tell what separates us from each other. The children are all improving. I have watched very closely the influences about them all, and as far as possible helped to arrange with you for their comfort and progress. I feel to assure you that there never was a time when the spirits were so close to the earth-life as now, and when they were so positive in their control of man. This will be seen ere long in much that they will do. You have gone on in advance of many minds, and you will see and gain as your reward much that has been promised you from time to time, giving you the strength and wisdom which above all things is the most to be coveted. Do not be sad about anything, but look away with me into the beautiful realities which we know exist everywhere about us. Let us be more and more closely united, while all the links which bind us together will continue to grow stronger and more bright. I am happy in all that you do to promulgate our beautiful philosophy. There will be many things given yet more startling than even those you have heard or witnessed. Do not think that mistakes or seeming incongruities put us away from you. No, we draw still nearer to bless with love which you know cannot fail. Dear B—— is growing manly and more beautiful each day. Bless you all with love. From your own loving wife with the circle,

FANNY.

MY DEAR FATHER—I am most anxious to have you feel at all times that I am with you, and that when the circle is formed about you we always give to our dear mother the first opportunity of writing to you. I will assist you in a variety of ways, and you will do the work which the world so much needs. The present fall and winter will be one of marked progress in the spiritual, and you will not suffer. On the contrary you will enjoy and rejoice in the truths which will continue to flow out through you. Our influence will go with you, softening and beautifying all that you meet, working and rejoicing that the shackles can and do fall from the souls of those who are still in bondage. Do not fear, dear father. We know all, and you will see the power of your loving ones with

ANNA.

Good evening, my dear husband. I know that you are ready to meet me, and we in turn just as happy to greet you. * * * You have yet much, very much to do, and while you work on in the truth you will gather a constant power which will go with you in each and every life duty. Have then no fears, no sorrows. I want you to be sure and speak out the truth to all whom you feel can accept it. You will be filled up with the influences of a circle who have humanity's good at heart, and all your children will eventually labor through you to create the highest and best conditions for your complete progress. Do not allow aught to disturb your thoughts of us as you go onward and forward in the truth. There is everything to encourage in the things of the present, and all the shadows seem to be passing away. I feel that the angels are drawing nearer to the earth-life, and I know that you will realize how perfectly all things will harmonize when the spirits are better acquainted with the world. I am so happy to assure you that all is moving orderly and well, and that the angels are never weary with watching.

In love, as ever, your own happy spirit-wife,
FANNY M. H.

DEAR FATHER—It was very kind of you to aid the spirits to-night, and to bring others forward to the altar, where they could begin on the ladder of spiritual progress to gain glimpses of the beautiful life which is in reality everywhere about them. Do not think or say that it is afar off—I mean the spirit-world; nay, it is only the upper half of your own, and you are all the time surrounded by the glad host who delight to linger near and bless you. I am not sorry that you taught me how to realize the presence of my mother, and I know that you can feel to-day that we are not separated, and that you can see, hear and almost feel our spiritual bodies near you. We can rise with your clearer vision into truths which are so palpable to you that they have become almost a part of yourself, and you cannot by any manner or mode of reasoning remove yourself from the best and pleasantest thought of all, namely, that you will join us here in the abode of the spirit, where our home is as tangible and more beautiful than any earth-home can be. Do not be uneasy about brother or G., or any of the loved ones, for they are all in our care, and we draw nearer to them when fear or sorrow attracts us. Do not think your winter will be dull or unhappy. All that we promise we will do, and as our influence increases, we will gather all the power to impress you to do our work through you. Mary is with me and the home circle, with your own ANNA.

MY DEAR HUSBAND—I am very happy to be with you this morning, and as you made the way for me to come, I have done so, bringing with me the happy circle which have congregated to cheer and bless you, making you to go forward in the earth-life and meet its strange changes with a degree of content which you could not gain without us. There are many things we wish you to know and feel in common with us. We make for you the basis of your own impressions, which we see will lead you where you can at all times be your own best medium. I am glad that you are with me in all things of truth and love. I want you to know that our years of happiness made for us both, and indeed for all, the happier state which now rests eternal and forever with us. I see our children all acting out a certain life-destiny, and each accepting that which belongs to them as individual lives.

E. has a firm, clear perception of the spiritual, and seems to live it in her own way. F. tries very hard to put it all aside, and rather studies to do so, at the same time believing, if so I may say, that there is truth in it; and indeed I am sure that she would not willingly aver that we do not come to her nor that we do not impress her. However, as her life does not as yet need this confession of faith we will be content in seeing her just as she is, happy without it. I wanted to be nearer to you than ever while our dear boy was suffering as he was, and I may say is now. Do not feel to hurry him to return to the city. Let him go on quietly and slowly gaining strength, as he has lost a great deal. G. will be quiet alone. I think it is best for her to remain there. Anna will come, and the way will be prepared for us to bring a very peaceful influence with those who are there. I am glad that I can meet you, and I can see how fully and beautifully I can and do impress you. There are many here, very many, and they who come, some to witness the manifestations and some to speak to you, are all orderly and beautiful spirits. The more you sit the oftener they can come in your thoughts, and their way there is plain and easy to reach others. Oh, how beautiful is the scene around you this morning! so many congregate, all strong and harmonious, with your loving spirit-wife, FANNY.

There are many kind friends here, and, as you know, mother has brought in some of her friends; of course the circle has become greatly enlarged and made happier by the presence of many spirits. You are blest, dear father, with the kindly influences of many who are with you at all times, and as your years go by you will feel still more of the presence of your devoted circle with your children. Father, dear, I shall be your housekeeper in your absence, and that, you know, means that I shall take good care of G. and B. There is need of my presence there, not because of any danger, but from the fact that I see in our presence a more harmonious influence. Be of good cheer, then, and know that all is safe.
ANNA.

I must greet you, friend, now that the way is open for me. I have no apology to make. Seeing became believing, and accordingly I am here with you, and very happy. Your wife and children were the first to attract me, and I find no difficulty now in being present sometimes to aid in the great cause; yet I know that I am weak and feeble compared to many. Your life and mine may differ, but both of us are spirits, under different covering. I thank you for the attraction. R. B. M.

Good morning, my dear friend. I came this morning to meet you, because I felt that you would be glad to hear from me, and accordingly I have entered. The spirit-life is indeed beautiful, and I am very happy in it. Not far away do I seem, but here, in the midst of a beautiful circle, who are ready, did the medium hold out, to write all day. Do not forget me, but accept me as an old friend. LEWELLYN HASKELL.

My son, take our greeting this bright, electric morn, and know that we come in love and gladness to bless thee. I have not been so far away but that, with thy father and friends, I have met thee with many kind and social hearts and seen thy life affecting those who before had felt that thee was deluded. Fear not the future, but move on in peace and harmony with thy kindred and loved ones ever the same. Grandfather is here, and Enoch. They are helping thee on with thy business, and they will live in thy life, aiding thee in every way. Bless thee, my child, ever and ever with thy father and mother.

MY DEAR HUSBAND—We are glad to meet you this morning, and purposely held you that we might continue in the same train of thought and communication that we left before. There is great joy in this pleasant intercourse between us, and we feel more happiness than do you, for you are all the time looking about you, and have to be interested in the material things of earth, and there are those events and circumstances which make up the sum of life; but when all is gone, and the full life of the affections is opened through the spiritual, then it is that we turn to that plane of life which will create for us the heaven which so many dream of, and yet know not how to reach. One by one the gentler influences of life come in and make up for us a thought by which we are attracted, and as faith increases we find the means to become more the substance than the shadow. I want you to live in the same love life that I do, and I cannot have you with me unless your spirit constantly draws me in the same ratio that I attract you. Be happy in whatever state you may be, and let all disappointment go by without making an impression upon your spirit. I would like so much to meet you at Moravia again, and will at the proper time. You will be impressed when to go, and will move along in harmony with the thoughts of the circle, who want most of all to greet you again. I have done many, many things for you, but I am ready to say that there never was a time when I felt so strong to do as now. I will hold you all, and the home-life will be glad and bright. I do not want the children to go in this steamer (of 20th Dec.). Others say that there is no danger, but I confess to having fears even here. G. is very well, F. is a little disappointed, but it will turn out wisely. B. is improving slowly, and his hand will be weak some time. Be careful of him. I want him to go abroad another year. Dear boy, how I love to gather with others of our circle, to bless you all, and him particularly, who so much needs me. Be as ever faithful and loving, and know me your own devoted FANNY.

Father dear, we come to gladden your lonely life with our bright presence, made the more beautiful because of your faith linking you so closely to us. Be sure of our presence, and do not think that we are away in the hours when you most need us. I want you to feel that we are with you, and will be this winter at home. Miss Sprague (Achsa) is with me, and many old friends, glad to join with you. Your faith, dear father, attracts many, and all that can come will do so. They who are learning to communicate find a helping hand through me, and one ready to receive and make welcome in yourself. I shall be with the dear ones in their journey, and the way will be made pleasant for you all at home and elsewhere. Do not think that we ask too much by urging or at least hoping that you will go again to Moravia. The time is rapidly approaching when these manifestations will be common everywhere and the materializing power will be at hand in every household of faith. Remember, dear father, we go with you always in love. Your happy circle, with ANNA.

MY DEAR FRIEND—I had hoped to meet you at Moravia. I think you would recognize me. I shall rejoice when there are more offices open to the preparation of the right kind of magnetism for us to appear face to face. I shall not forget my promise to you, and will come with your circle to cheer and brighten your spirit. Do not think there is a falling off of these manifestations; on the contrary, they are expressing themselves everywhere, according to the development of those to whom they come. I trust you are aware of the magnet* which attracts your friend
ACHSA SPRAGUE.

*Her portrait, hanging in my library, which was placed there by her express request, made from the spirit-life.

MY DEAR HUSBAND—I am with you this morning, and I know that you need not to be told of the circle which at all times surround and aid your spirit on the path of life and duty. You will have to be patient about our dear sister. She is coming in her own way, and will come to you from the home she inhabits. Do n't be over anxious—wait and be patient. Isabella came this morning, with others, and was anxious to speak to you. And as all should at least have that privilege I try to aid them. She is a beautiful spirit, full of kind acts, and our dear children gather about her, ready to accept her love and guidance. I want you to encourage our dear ones each and all. I am delighted to see B. so well pleased and pleasing others. Have no fears in regard to him. A kind, loving spirit (Achsa Sprague) goes forth with you and is keeping her promise with you. She will guard our dear boy from temptation and danger, and comes with the loving sisters to bless you all.

I know that you will understand our aid, and feel that you are helped and not arbitrarily dictated to by us. In all things of the earth interested we must be, for we are not separated, and you are helping us to make more beautiful this habitation of the Father's love. Bless you, my dear one; and know that as ever I am your own loving spirit-wife, FANNY.

MY DEAR FATHER—Two grandmothers deputed me to express their tender care and greater love. Dear, blessed father, how I love to cheer and gladden your heart with these evidences of the kindly guidance of those who are so closely allied to you. I know how your spirit goes out to us, and we seem at times to journey off together in the beautiful home. I am happy in all the relations of the earth-life, and to each and all, with or without their consent, we go to speak words of love or encouragement. Be of good cheer, dear father, and know that there is constant development with you, and we are anxious to lessen your cares so that we can be more constantly with you, opening your vision to behold more of the glories of the beautiful home where we shall enjoy many blissful seasons together. In love, your own

ANNA, *with the Circle.*

MY DEAR FRIEND—You have afforded me great pleasure in accepting me just as I was. It is rather difficult for a man to own to error in life when there are so many around trying to bolster him up and keep every one else out, as the church did and does. I am glad to be of sane mind here and see for myself. Your wife brought me. I saw her and yourself together, and was happy in that one truth, for I knew it was real. I shall gain strength and do my work; yet it is no small thing for a man like myself to throw off a lifelong belief. But when it holds you from the joys beyond and before you, there is nothing else to do. I have many kindred here, but they do not advance as yet. They will when they dare to. I am ROBERT B. MINTURN.

MY DEAR BROTHER—I come to please Fanny, Anna and the others, but I still have my doubts whether I do this or the medium. I was with Fanny at that place where you saw her (Moravia). I wish I could know if it is really true, and whether it is dangerous to believe it or not. What do you think? I will try and be honest with you, but I don't believe it is all right. Will you excuse me, and believe if you can that it is

AGATHA?

MY FRIEND—I do not come to you to-day to talk about business, save as it is presented in the general outlook. Delay and suspension of all things pertaining to business will continue until what is rotten is weeded out, and a better foundation laid politically, socially and religiously. We have nothing to do but to look on and operate upon the minds of individuals, creating as far as possible individual reform and individual strength to resist the evil which has overwhelmed a nation in its haste to grow rich. The spirit-world has been filled with influences which have had great attraction to the earth, whither they have returned to outwork the life and satisfy the ambitions which were the leading features of their earthly career. There can be but little progress in the earth-life until a better class of spirits leave their mortal bodies. If they who would do good whilst on earth would begin aright, they would enjoy themselves vastly more when they get here and find a wider field for doing good. So few understand the real and the true life, and there is so much to learn and to do in every day's duty as it comes and goes, that men should and will ere long learn that they are in a school-room where there are instructors who teach the soul to understand and know more of its individual self. The whole basis of life is wrong, from the fact that there is no truth in the educational idea that man starts out with, namely, that his soul either passes at once on its exit into heaven or into eternal punishment. I can hardly understand from my present standpoint how it is that the world has continued so long in this bondage.

Theodore Parker and others are here to-day waiting to be recognized by you, hence I will not hold the medium longer. ROBERT,
With Rowland and William (Minturn).

———

Yes, my friend, we are capable of doing more than some give us credit for. We roam with all faithful hearts, particularly with those we find ready to speak out and own the truth as it was and is in all great lives, from Confucius to Jesus of

Nazareth, and from the latter to the present day, and in all time. So will it be in eternity, the portals of which are open to every living soul, God calling all to come in and witness of himself in his own holy temple, namely, his own children.

I prophesy to you a remarkable season near at hand. Strange conflicts of mind and thought, battles in which right will sweep away might with bloodless victory, *spirit* rule the *letter* and mankind draw nearer to God the Father. Bless you, old friend.   THEODORE PARKER.

MY BROTHER—I have been at this place before with you, but did not gain sufficient power over the medium to express myself to you. Robert came with the circle that now surrounds you, and seemed to lead the way. It is pleasant to be recognized, and a beautiful boon to be able to keep up the interests and friendships which a life of strange vicissitudes creates. I loved Fanny, as you knew, and I tell you here that I felt sad to part with her. Something told me that it was the last time I should see her in the earth-life. Hence why I returned so early to her. I am glad that you have startled with that statement* those who

---

*[From the New York World, Feb. 1, 1873.]
On the 12th day of October, 1838, I was united in wedlock with Miss Frances Minturn (now deceased), daughter of the late Jonas Minturn, of New York City. In about a week after we took passage (accompanied by two of my own sisters) in the packet-ship Quebec, Captain Hibbard, for London, where we arrived, *via* Portsmouth, in about twenty days. Rowland R. Minturn, the eldest brother of my wife, to whom she and all the other members of the family were, not without manifold reasons, idolatrously attached, accompanied us to Sandy Hook, where he left to return with the pilot apparently in good health and spirits. After passing a few days in London, we proceeded to Paris (*via* Dover and Boulogne), where we stayed about a month, when I purchased a carriage, in which we traveled post to Rome by way of Lyons, Marseilles, Toulon, Nice, the Maritime Alps, and Genoa.

Although we were in constant receipt of letters from home bearing cheerful tidings, my wife expressed fears even before we left Paris that we should hear unpleasant news from her relatives in New York. As we journeyed on, her forebodings increased, although all the letters that

regard us as *inert* and beyond the reach of mortal progress.

Speaking of business, I think that R. B.—who were forwarded by our bankers were of the most satisfactory character. By the time we had passed the mountainous region and descended into the valley of the Rhone, her morbid feelings became so intensified that she ceased to take interest in the beauties that were constantly presenting themselves. It was in vain I represented to her that every letter we had received from home was full of cheering news. Her spirit became more and more depressed, and by the time we reached the Alps, I became so affected myself through sympathy or some unexplainable cause, that I could not get rid of a very unpleasant feeling of doubt in regard to home matters. Her family consisted of a mother, four brothers, and four sisters, but about this time her forebodings seemed to take more definite shape and centre on her brother Rowland. The night we arrived at Genoa, on suddenly awakening I found her sitting up in bed, sobbing bitterly. On asking her why she wept, she told me that her brother Rowland had just appeared to her in a dream, looking pale and death-like. Although not at ease myself on the subject, I endeavored to persuade my wife that the dream was caused by her own excited imagination. She finally became more composed and I fell asleep, but only to be awakened again by similar tearful lamentations, while she vehemently affirmed that her brother Rowland must be dead, as he had again appeared to her looking as he did before, with one hand raised and pointing upward. After this fearful night it was difficult to induce my wife even to look out the carriage window at any of the admirable works of art or nature with which Italy abounds. On our arrival at Rome, we took rooms at the Russian Hotel, and engaged a hack or carriage and a suitable driver for a month, that we might visit the objects of interest in and around the city. My wife accompanied us in our daily drives in one or two instances, but took no note of the objects of general interest, and feeling that the sacrifice was painful to her, we forbore pressing her to accompany us. As her feelings became more and more morbid, I generally declined accompanying my sisters in their drives, and remained at home. On my awakening one morning, I found my wife again weeping, when, in answer to my inquiries, she told me that her brother Rowland had just appeared to her again, looking all pale and death-like, with his finger pointing upward as he did at Genoa. For some particular reason I accompanied my sisters that day on their accustomed drive. On our return, my wife was sitting on a sofa looking even more distressed than usual, and pointed to a letter lying on the table that had been left by the postman. I hastily broke the seal, and, catching a glimpse of the signature, joyfully exclaimed, "Why, Fanny, it is from your brother Rowland." But in turning to its commencement I soon found that it conveyed the tidings of that brother's sudden and unexpected death, announced by his cousin, the late Robert B. Minturn, the similarity of whose signature had for a moment misled me.

THOMAS R. HAZARD.

Vaucluse, R. I., Jan. 24th, 1873.

is here with me—and myself will be able to aid you. But do not suppose that we are infallible. We are not, and are liable to make great mistakes, from the one cause that we see into the minds of a few persons to whom we are attracted, and judge from what is passing in them what will be the result in a given case, whereas it not unfrequently happens that other minds interested that we have not looked into come up and overpower or control those we have seen. You must therefore watch with care. We are happy, and subscribe ourselves your friends and kindred,

R. R. M.
R. B. M. } (*Minturn.*)

QUERY—(*Addressed to R. B. M.*) When on earth you were an earnest friend of the clergy and the church. What are your ideas now?

"On all sides, church and theology are like the garments that one wears in their day and style. When laid aside, they laugh at the absurdity of such fashions. I see the church now as it is, no longer through a glass darkly. I have met Bishop Delancy, Dr. Hawks, and a number of others here that were known to me in life."

(QUERY)—"Those who have the least to unlearn, are happiest and freest here. The one who is crushed by circumstances that he or she sighs in vain to remove, rises into a happier state, and is at rest in the fulness of that light and life which is no longer dimmed by man's authority. Rowland is here, peaceful and harmonious. I see your family, and I thank them for the kindness which has brought me hither.

Your friend, R. B. MINTURN."
(*fac simile.*)

MY DEAR HUSBAND—We have gathered our forces to meet you this morning, and are as ever ready to impart the strength which I know you are in need of not only to brighten and lighten

life's journey, but to give to your spirit the power to go forth and do good to others. I am not surprised at your efforts, and know that you can gain only by keeping at work. I say at work, and yet I know it is impossible to keep still or to know how much good you do, for like all seed that has fallen on hard ground no one can tell when it will spring up or what fruit it will bear. Our labor is one of continued love, and we *cannot* if we *would* separate ourselves from those we love. We are looking over all the things of earth-life together, and as we move on in the same ratio we are made much happier to know that all the beautiful realities of our home here are but living over again all that has made us happy in the earthly home. I know your anxieties and your thoughts, and I can only say to you that you need not fear. The promises made to guard our children are all sacredly kept, and the band which surrounds you will ever be the same, faithful and loving, with your own
FANNY.

MY DEAR FATHER—I am glad to meet you where I can speak so plainly to you. I see this medium so accessible to all that you attract that it is like being in the midst of a multitude of sounds and only a few leading words can be given. Yet believe me, dear father, we all do the best we can, and when all things are considered it is a wonder we do as much as we do. One thing is certain: we always help, direct, and guard you from danger. With tenderest love, your
ANNA.

We will meet you at home, my friend, and will help you to know my presence. In all that you do, fear not, but live as ever in the truth. I will write you from your own mediumship, or rather from your own impressions, when you will let me. I only want the opportunity to do so, and I know that our united influence will tell many things which the world is reaching out for. Never think, my friend, that your labor is lost, or that what you do amounts to but little in this cause. Be assured that it will be well received and well recorded in the home where good deeds make the habitation of the spirit more beautiful. Your friend, ACHSA SPRAGUE.

MY GOOD FRIEND—You need not wonder at the pressure of thought which sometimes seems to open to you volumes of truth and glorious revelations. To you who have dared to speak the truth a host is constantly appealing, and if at times they conflict, believe it to be by the same law which attracts and holds the myriad atoms in space together. We are anxious to find you at leisure, and have promised to be orderly and not overtax you if you will allow us to give our truths to the world through you. There never was so great a demand for all the truths which we desire to give as now, and you will not, I trust, blame us if we seem to be impatient. I am glad to be with you, and shall never be able to express the joy that we feel when recognized and accepted by friends who are willing to receive our presence. Kindly, W. C. and T. P.
(*Wm. Channing and Theodore Parker.*)

We are happy in every development of the spiritual, and no men need wonder at our giving them power to act if they have a desire so to do. Our ways are different from yours, and men need not be regarded as fanatics because of their not following out the beaten path even of the Spiritualist. The better proof of spirit-communion lies in the variety of its manifestations to different persons. All proof of identity and individual progress lies in this variety, and without it we could not be to you what we were in life. I have a series of chapters which I want to present to you sooner or later through some medium (I am not particular who, provided they are adapted to us,) on the capacity or varieties of media. It is high time this whole question was better understood, for we certainly desire to keep Spiritualism out of sectarian lines, through the teachings of media who draw sectarian influences. I want you to consider this, and we will agree to furnish the matter with your many friends. Excuse this interpolation, and believe me your friend, J. P. (*John Pierpont.*)

My Dear Father—I am most happy to meet you here this morning, and, as you know, delighted to be where I can bring another evidence of my presence with you. I know that you are not in need of tests, and that you find yourself happiest in the evidence which you are enabled to gain through the impressions which I make upon your spirit direct, for in thoughts of me I am constantly holding sweet converse with you. The whole circle have gathered and will bless you, as ever, with the magnetism which helps to make stronger your body, soul and spirit. I am happy to be here, and am ever your loving child. Dr. Grinnell is trying to come to you here, and anxious to draw some of the old spirits to prove to you even more than he gave while with you. Come, dear father, talk with us and let us hold sweet communion together. Mother and all the dear ones have joined you here to answer some of the questions which you are most anxious to know, and we love to see your thoughts in harmony with us while we journey on almost unmindful of the change which you call death. Dear father, we have no thoughts apart from you. There is no separation, and your spirit is just as fully in the spirit-home with us *now* as it ever can be. Full of love, and ever your own,
ANNA.

My Dear Father—I have met Doctor Grinnell many times at your circle, and as you are well aware, there were moments when he did not realize nor believe that those ancient spirits came to him. He is anxious now to tell you that the realities of the spirit-life are far more beautiful and wonderful than he could with his peculiar organization have believed. He is thankful to you for your faith and perseverance, and is ready as ever to reach afar into the circles, if I may so say, of doubt and darkness, and bring them forward to the light which will cheer and brighten the path of progress. I saw you with B., and I am happy with him in his effort to go forth in the busy life and discipline of the material, and I have no fears of his going very far astray. I am happy in all that you do for our children, and I know that you will see our power in all that you do. Perhaps we should qualify our expression and say that your spirit enjoys much, and is in reality with us in many things that are not manifest to the material senses. There is nothing that I cannot help you to gain or to do, and although I may appear slow and tedious, it nevertheless comes along in good time, and all are better satisfied for having had the experience and discipline which brings progress. You will have a pleasant winter, and so will the children. Do not think that there are to be no shadows. They will come, and they at all times ripen the fruits that are made more perfect by storm, sunshine and shade. I have much to say to you on many points, and I know that you will fully understand us. Come, talk to us, husband and father, for all have gathered, and even now we are trying to point or make plain to you these gardens of perennial bloom, whose fragrance reaches you from out the beautiful gate we shall some day open to you. Your own FANNY, MARY and ANNA.

Good morning, my dear ones. I brought you here this morning that I might enjoy a social chat with you. I find that our influence will reach you at any point, but I know that you are happier when we can bring to you the evidences which make you to feel that it is indeed your loving circle. B. has not been homesick as yet, and he will not be, for there are so many about him to make him feel at home that he will not know or feel the absence of those at home. I am delighted with the place you are in, my dear B., and I regard it as every way adapted to your tastes and capacities. Be, as ever, full of good hope and good feeling. You will not meet with many obstacles or difficulties, but will enjoy the happier condition, which will enable you to meet all things without fear or dread. Be content to draw upon yourself for all that you need, for in self-reliance come impressions which will individualize and strengthen you all the way through life. Be sure and keep passive, yet firm, and by no means allow fear to come into your spirit. I know the question arises, How can you do all this? To which I reply, If you take proper care of your diet, and live regularly in all things, you will have made the conditions to draw us nearer and nearer to you. Do not permit yourself to be looking away into the future for your happiness, but of all things cultivate the frame of thought which will enable you to enjoy the present.

Anna is with me, and all the loving ones. You will go to the dear old home soon, and we shall have a happy summer. All of us will meet you there. Say to your sisters that I am watchful and faithful as ever to them. I try to make them understand me, and I know that they do recognize me in all that I do for them. I see no shadows, no sorrows, that our faith and influence will not overcome. I will be with you, and you will know that I am aiding you. Your father is full of faith, and we help to strengthen it with every thought and impulse. Grandfather is here, and uncle, and we must not take up all the time, but will give to each an opportunity, as we have had, to express love and kindness. I am so happy to see each one and all of you resting on the light of truth and feeling—that freedom which at all times creates progress! I do not come to dictate or to tell of material things, but to aid as far as possible in all that will make life peaceful and useful. Your sisters are going to be well and happy, and I can see you united under the influence of the happy spirit-circle. Love in abundance to all from the other half of the family, who are never separated from the love of those who exist in the material life. There is no break in the great chain of love, and I know that as you grow older the more you will realize the fact that we are and ever must be one united family, made happier by the knowledge of our continued union. I hardly know how to relinquish the pencil, yet I know that you will forgive if I have appeared selfish.

Always lovingly,
Your faithful wife, and mother,
FANNY.

My son, we cannot come to thee with tests that will startle and make thee curious to seek out more of the marvelous. There is nothing so marvelous as the simpler things of nature, and thee can study there and find thy best evidences of spirit power in the earth. I have lost my desire to hold on to earthly treasure, and have decided to go forth with thee and help do good in the earth. Do not wonder that so much is expected of thee when thy mind and thy spirit has been opened to understand material things. The great Father demands that of those who have, much shall be demanded. Now all that I see for thee is to give out in speech, in act and in thy whole life, so that when the gateway opens, and that entrance so long promised to spiritual things, then shall thy voice help to swell the greater cloud of witnesses about thee. Oh, how I long to see thee helping thy kindred into paths of peace and righteousness. Thy grandfather,
T. H.

I meet you this morning, the appointment being made by ourselves. We are always ready to fulfill, it being a great pleasure to us, and perhaps we shall never be able to know all of the joys which are in store for us until we meet here, where the spirit will put on more of its real life, and enjoy still more of the glories which the great and loving Father has in store for those who desire to know more of him. The blessing of Spiritualism, my dear one, is not confined to the few conditions of life. That taught us in our youth served for a few emergencies, and we hardly dare to feel that it was possible to draw from the spiritual life more than that which was positively and absolutely required to hold us to our sectarian forms, for, plain as they were, we see them now as binding and restraining the spirit from its more full development. In this intercourse we find everything that the soul desires, and know that we can ask no more, for material things will follow, and all these harmonies will be felt about us. We know not how much good we can do if we only know how to do it. Spirits teach how to do good! That is the highest mission of spirits. We always preach to you, and often use up much of the time in that way, but it is of some importance to be able to tell others that Spiritualism reaches every demand of the body, soul and spirit. Be sure, my dear one, to continue in faith, truth and love. I know that you will, and in being *that*, you will be all things. I want you to be sure and tell them all at home that I shall be there plainer and more palpable than ever during the coming summer. As we gain strength we will make such manifestations as will be best adapted to the care and comfort of home. Fear not, but be quiet and happy in yourself, and so shed out from the soul and spirit all that the angels bring to you. There are a number of spirits now about you, and I see that many are anxious to write you. I am delighted with the place and progress which B. is enjoying, and I shall through you convey light, life and strength to all our children. I see their thoughts, and know their needs, and through you will help them to a peaceful and useful life on earth, so that when they enter here they will have finished the duties of the earthly sphere, and enjoy the reward which is before them. We are all here, but it may not be possible for us all to write. We shall be with you in all that you do, and you will know your faithful wife, children, and many friends all in the circle of truth and love, with your faithful wife, FANNY.

I did not mean to intrude upon others, but I cannot let you go without saying a few words about home in the spirit and home in the earth-life. We are all happy in watching over your spiritual life and progress, and in seeing all that is near and dear to you made beautiful and holy, thus giving you back a harvest of rich faith annexed with constant evidences of more power and strength of the intercourse that is so rapidly spreading all over the world. Father dear, I have much to tell you, and in good time you shall know more of our beautiful home, and how we pass the time. Sit in a circle at home. A. S. will go with me there, and you will know our united care over all the dear ones. Dear father, when I look out upon the earth-life, and mingle with it, I almost long to be back again where I can do more good, and inspire humanity to be more faithful, truthful and loving to each other, and thus draw nearer to God, and live in the love which belongs to the spirit. I love to linger near my dear brother, and aid him in the life duties. Pure, beautiful and good, we bless him always in love and peace. We are always your loving children, ANNA and MARY.

It is well, my dear husband, to make an engagement and come to keep it, from the fact that it prepares us to be here to meet you. There are many spirits around this morning, who, having known that you were to be here, entered before us to await your coming. We see that you are prepared for us, and that charges the medium with the influence that we can control, sometimes, advantageously, and again we find it difficult to do more than say a few words. The more there are gathered the less you get, for in the combination of influences there is always disorder; not because the spirits desire to make it, but from the fact that the medium is unable to work it off. Spirits fail often in their estimate of what a medium is capable of doing, and many times are called unreliable when they are not aware of having failed in what they were desirous of doing. I see so many in this state that I cannot but speak of it to you. One might as well suppose that an absent one heard every thought and motion as to suppose that friends in the body hear, see and feel much that spirits do or try to manifest to earth friends. I have the children with me this morning, and my father and mother, with your own, form part of the group which surround you. We have talked to you of business matters, and while, as I have before said, we do not like to dictate, we enjoy talking with you and helping you to move safely in your business affairs. We see and know much that you do, but not all. When you sit down and reflect, then we come to you, and you know our influence, which comes to strengthen or weaken impressions which you have. All the dear ones are doing well, and I trust you are fully aware of our influence over and with them. Do not feel that there are any changes we would ask that we cannot give to you. There are many things for you to do in life, but whatever you do it is our wish to make easy rather than burdensome to you. I want you to rest and enjoy yourself as far as you can, for I know there are many pleasant years before you, and the children certainly need the most of your time and care, for around you we can draw all our united influences of love and truth. Do not weary in well-doing, and always act as aware of

our presence and our guardian care. You will have a pleasant trip, and it will do you good to meet and mingle with your friends in the body as well as out. B. is well and happy. Have no fears of him. Our love can shelter and render him peaceful and harmonious. We can walk by his side, and help him to shed an influence on and over others which will be every way profitable, keeping him from temptation and making him strong in truth and virtue. Oh, how I love to come into our home and find there the welcome of love and truth, to impart the health-giving power of spirit intercourse and continuous love, such as mothers feel, and then to have it intensified by the passing through that which we were wont to fear and dread. Always in love, your faithful wife, FANNY,
With loving children and friends.

Much that I did not believe, although it came through myself, is now made plain to me. Oh, how I long to fill mediums with a greater knowledge of their usefulness and power! I have tried the realities of the eternal world, and when I see the many spirits reaching out to be helped and to help others, I feel that I have a greater work to do than ever before. You know, my friend, belief has passed into sight, and I know now that I live and am an intelligent spirit. Help me to do good, and give me some chance to teach others how great is the power of the spirit-world over mortals. I am DR. J. GRINNELL.

Talk to us, friend; let us see if there is anything we can do for thee. We are the living ones, and men who heed not truth are the dead.
JOHN WOOLMAN.

MY DEAR HUSBAND—I was with you in the writing you were lately engaged in, and was par-

ticularly interested in your expressing yourself
so truthfully on all points that pertain to and
add weight to the testimony which is everywhere
going forth in the world. We see the truth now,
and have to live it and act in it, as the atmosphere about us requires each and every spirit to
come under the absolute control of the laws of its
own structure and quality. And as I go forward
in the development of the spirit life, I find that
the most perfect progress is in individualization.
That your life on earth and in the body is moving along in comparative ratio with our own, we
realize more fully, so much so indeed that I do
not consider myself separated from you. I know
that you ask through your own thoughts many
questions relative to our united lives. You wonder if the requirements of the body and material
demands separate you in any way from me.
Your spirit, my dear one, is developing through
all, and while your body was the machinery
through which your spirit manifested to my material senses I became more attached to you.
Understanding that the spiritual was an impos-
sibility without the manifestations and experiences which we had as mortals, I knew you better and loved you more as I became better acquainted with you in our lives together, and as
that ripened we became so permanently united
that my spirit could not be apart from your own.
Hence our progress together spiritually has made
for us both a deeper and more abiding love. I
am better pleased with our union now, from the
fact that we live and love to be in one circle. I
am most happy to tell you this, for I do assure
you that since I had that remarkable experience
at Moravia I have grown so strong that I can
feel my individual life and your own as one harmonious union, both acting a life of truth and
glory. I see many things of the material life,
but you know, my dear husband, they do not appear to me as they did in earth-life. Dear B. ! I
love to come into his spirit and life, and I cannot
fully realize that he is growing to manhood. On
the contrary, I enter into his life with the same

feeling of affection and fondness that I did when he was a child. He has a sweet spirit, and will be a good man, watched and guarded by the angels. I shall help them all, not dictating positively, but guarding them with a spirit-mother's love. You know that we have a large circle here. Our beautiful family gathers about me, and each one has some special department to attend to in the earth-life. My brother Rowland has been here with me several times, but whenever he has given his name the medium has thought it must be your living brother, and hence it has been difficult for him to speak to you. We do not leave you to-day beneath or out of our influence, but we do come nearer at all times when the spirit attracts and requires that guidance which only love and truth can bring. Be sure of this, and be strong, doing good, with the love of your own devoted FANNY.

DEAR FATHER—I must follow to-day, for the circle of home is full of strength and light shed out on every side to make more perfect their work through you. I trust that you are aware that any mention made of a spirit, publicly attracting attention to said spirit, draws them nearer to the earth-life. Uncle Rowland M. just begins to find his way here. He has been at other places, and now seems ready to take the pencil, and we will help to make up the more perfect influence for writing. I want you to accept all that your own spirit feels is truth, and we regard you in no danger as long as you work with the one blessed motive—namely, spreading the truth. I will help dear G., whom we all feel needs the most harmonious influences. There is a beautiful life all about you here to-day. All come with fresh garlands to bless your life with a portion of their own. Fear not, dear father; the knowledge which must cover the earth is that which comes in divine wisdom and love.
Your own happy,
ANNA, MARY and all.

Here we are face to face with those who love and bless you with more real fervor than all others left on earth. We do not worship afar off; we come right into your life, and speak to you with our hearts beating so close to your own that you do not longer ask if we are with you, for you know we are. I have grown stronger and stronger. As your faith has increased you see us in all that pertains to your own progress, and you realize how perfectly interested we are in the loved ones who have been spared to make your life gladsome. I shall be nearer to you each day, and you will not regret the time you have spent in the search for truth. I see the way is not so long now. You will come to my home some day, and the door will be opened to you long before your spirit realizes the fact that it has left the body. I am sure of your coming to me a glad, free, pure spirit. This is enough for me to know, and I do n't want you to think that your life-discipline is going to separate us. I see the children at home. Your presence will be welcomed, yet the kindly spirits who have promised to take care of the dear ones have been faithful, and will ever be the same loving ones. I shall see you safe to your home, and we will sit down together to worship and gain more of the life and beauty of our home eternal. The children are with me waiting to tell their care and love.

With affection, your wife,   FANNY.

DEAR FATHER—We have looked in upon you in your journeying, and seen how gladly you accepted all the evidences of our kindly care. We have spoken to you through thought, and tried to manifest at every place where a welcome was extended to us. Do not think you have had a single unprofitable moment. The way has been brightened by the presence of friends in and out of the body. You carry us with you wherever you go. I want you to remain as ever strong as the champion of those through whom the Great

Father sends truth. I shall be with you at home, and bring them all to welcome you. Many come to you whom you do not know. You have welcomed them in your own way, and bade them go forth on their missions of peace and good will to man. This makes you a medium of one kind, namely, to circulate the truth. I did so want to come and show myself, but I could not do so. You know that I am with you, and yet a little stronger evidence is always acceptable. You realize that the light of our home is the greatest attraction for us, and we join you there with the same unweaned love and tender care. With love enough for all, I am your own loving daughters,

ANNA and MARY.

MY DEAR LOVING FATHER—The tie which binds us to you cannot be severed. It matters not where you journey, there we find ourselves able to join you. I have long desired to speak to my dear brother at home, and have impressed him in my own way to know that I can guard and would protect him all through life, making his pathway peaceful and pleasant. I do n't want him to go out from home. I would keep him there ever and always. The dear old home is so precious to me that I want to see you always there in sweet council together. I perhaps would do him injustice and mar his progress, but I cannot endure the contact of mixed magnetism, and I am anxious to keep him from it. I see that his mind is to some extent unsettled. This is not to be wondered at when the outside world makes such a pressure upon him. I will be with him smoothing his pathway, and helping to make his life glad and beautiful. You, my dear father, have nothing to fear. The battle of life is well-nigh ended, and death can bring no terrors to you. F., G. and E. will be a comfort while you stay, and when we open wide the door to this life, where all the glories so long promised you meet your gaze, you will walk forward with that renewed strength and vigor which will make your spirit to rejoice in the full tide of praise and harmony. I sometimes grow impatient for the time to come; and yet I know we have no right to hasten the hours or wish them one less.

I shall be at home with you when you return. You will know me by your side with sisters and dear mother, beautiful and bright in the love which has never known a change. I am going now to see them at home. With love, your own
ANNA.

Well, Thomas, many friends come to add their testimony and to hold council with you. I need not tell you that spirits differ almost as much as mortals. One class comes to tell you that there is nothing alarming in the present situation, while another would impress you that there is danger on every side. Such confusion! leaving you to obey, as you should, your own impressions, and to give to your own judgment the most positive power! I know that all men are surrounded by spirits, each in their own way acting upon the brain as they best know how, that they may make you run into strange schemes sometimes, not for mischief, but from the fact that they want to be busy with material affairs, and try to hold communion with you and influence your thought in relation to what is to happen in the future, when in reality they know less of it than you do. Another class may see clearly a distant result, which will be so far in the future that telling it in advance may cause still greater mischief. Hence the better way, in my opinion, is to keep entirely harmonious and accept only that which accords with your own judgment. You know that when too many try to talk it makes confusion, and in the much that is said it is difficult to say which is right.

I am often with you, and will be known as ever your friend, R. B. M.

My Dear Husband—We were with you to-day in your search for the medium's new residence, and we made you feel encouraged to find it, so that we could talk to you freely. We know your thoughts, and look in upon your soul life as a part of your and our own happiness. There is one thing certain : we have made our life felt by all who will accept us, and we only ask acknowledgment of our presence and recognition of our kindly care. I find that our dear ones are looking from their own standpoint upon this our home and heaven, and while they are happy, each in their own way, be sure that they are made happier by the quiet guidance of our love and care. It matters not if they do not hear us with material ears, so long as the heart accepts and acts its teachings. F. cannot help her unbelief, and it is as natural to her to reject as it is for E. to receive. I see G. and B. each receptive, but in different ways. You will hear from them in their life of earth more of our guidance and discipline.

I am glad to meet you. Anna and the dear children all gather here to bless you, while the many loved ones of the circle are waiting to bless you with messages of truth and love.

Your own, ever, Fanny.

And I, too, my dear father, am very glad to meet you ; and I could not give up the search for the medium, so happy are we when we can find a channel through which we can speak to the loved of earth. Oh, my dear father, if mediums only knew how great is the reward of those who move on faithful and true, regardless of what materiality says or does, truly there would be no such sadness, no such fear as we so often see in the hearts of the weary. We come with pity and offer our friendship, which, when they understand, they will not think of so little value. The time is not distant when they who are faithful will have their reward, and a better class of

Spiritualists will rise up to protect and bless those to whom they must go to have the door opened to a better home. I know that a season of rest is near for those who need our care, and the many who have been faithful will have all that has been promised. I want you to be as ever their champion, and let them feel that in you they will ever have a friend. I go with a circle who are mediums, and their words are words of comfort. You know that Achsa Sprague has promised you to keep guard over sisters and brother, and she will keep her word. Spiritualism has now so firm a footing that it cannot go back, nor will it change its onward course if all the mediums should prove untrue. There are circles of wisdom who control all; even those afar up come, and in the spirit of truth and justice they give forth to those who hand out to media, and when they see that a medium has begun to allow the control of a lower order of spirits who are in the sphere of power they very soon confound them. Hence a medium's tricks (so-called) should be evidence only that there are all kinds of spirits ready to control mortals who are open to them. Your way has been consistent and judicious, and hence you have ever and always had consistent spirits to communicate with. We come at home and speak to you in and through thought, and will help to arrange a peaceful, happy summer. We see many of your friends gathered, and many who desire to talk often press around, unable to communicate. Do not feel that we can ever forget or leave you. No, my dear father, although our home is beautiful here, it is made happier by the knowledge of your one day coming to complete its joys. G. is better. B. is stronger, body and spirit. F. is happy in her way. All are dear to us, and to your own happy ANNA.

My friend, let me say to you that he or she who thinks that the day of restitution and the revolution which came has done its work and is over, is laboring under a most fatal mistake. This is the beginning of a day of judgment, and the strong hand of justice is abroad. We will work with you, and will add a strength and nerve to our councils which will bring justice and equity into the foundation of government, for it is at the very head of the nation that we would commence. T. PARKER.

MY DEAR HUSBAND—I came here with you to-day, and have made the way for you to sit down with me while I could rest your spirit and make you feel that we were as ever together and happy in our own way, quietly communing in thought and feeling, the same. We know that you are always receptive, and always ready to move with us in and through the different inspirations which come to lift you out of all sorrow and regret, afar into the spirit-life. How pleasant it is to join our thoughts. I must say so, for I cannot think of anything more closely allied than are the spirits of two who move in unison and in oneness as we do. We have our children, it is true, and they make a common bond and interest in which we find ourselves living over our own lives. Then again, we live in ourselves apart from all else, so individualized that we can continue to progress, and to grow nearer to each other, so that we have only to be happy and glad. I see our children in the form, each working out their life according to their own spiritual strength and being. I have longed to show you in my own way how they were placed spiritually, but have failed to do so, from the fact that it is almost impossible to describe surroundings that are so peculiarly spiritual. As I see them, F. is a medium of strong powers, and yet fails ofttimes to obey the higher control of those who are about her for her own great good. She tries to reason herself into unbelief, and in so doing comes into direct contact with the proofs of spirit communion. I have seen her so positively under the control of her sisters, who are with me, that she has been all day acting in the material mechanically, while in the spirit she has been with them. As for G., she is more than medium, and until the outside powers overpowered us I was satisfied of her great mediative power, to control which would have been an easy matter, only for her allowing her nervous system to have been so fearfully overpowered by that repeated and prolonged operation on her teeth. You may think strange of my speaking of this, but I cannot restrain myself from doing so to-day. I want you to understand that there are many things that are problems to me, and I sometimes think that you know more than I do even about spiritual things. You draw from the many whom you see and I see, and mingle with the few who are congenial to me. Hence many things that I want to know I come to you to learn. I cannot think that G. will ever suffer again as in the past. E. is impressional, and her passivity makes her very accessible to a high order of spirits. Anna delights to be near and with her. B. is our gentle and beautiful child. His life is one of joy to himself; his thoughts are so peaceful and pleasant, and his whole being is so filled with our own affection and harmony, that nothing remains but for him to be peaceful and happy in himself, and a joy to others as well. My brothers are with me to-day. I see and feel their magnetism here with you. Then I have my sisters with me, but not always, for as in earth-life they have other attractions, and bend to them. We are, however, harmonious together, and very peaceful. I want you to feel that I am happiest when with you, and that whatsoever pleases you adds to my happiness. The discipline of the earth-life with its material appetites and needs does not come into my sphere, nor is my magnetic power disturbed by anything that you do. We live as one in spirit, faithful and true. Your own loving FANNY.

MY DEAR, PRECIOUS FATHER—Your presence at the room of a medium is the signal for all who know you. We glide in as if beckoned from afar, and our feet make haste to be with you again. Dear, blessed father, we look into your heart and see your spirit's needs. It is enough for us to see that you are still faithful to our truths, and that your heart is always open to accept us. It makes no difference what the outside world thinks or says of us. We live in our own world with you, and that world is so joyous—oh, so joyous, to those who realize and enjoy it as we do! Our friend, dear Achsa, is a beautiful spirit, bright and electric, who lights up our circle with a newer and a brighter joy when you call us together. I am so happy to be in your thoughts, as one not gone, but present with you! Sister Mary is with me, and the many dear ones who gather to cheer. With love to the dear ones at home and to yourself, always the same loving circle, with your daughters,

ANNA and MARY.

MY DEAR FRIEND—You are looking about you, to gain, as far as possible, some knowledge of the future, as well as to satisfy yourself that all *is well* in the present. I am very glad that you understand me as one who has gone only a little way before you, and who fully realizes all the beauty of the great world upon which he has entered. I know that spirits have to learn a great deal, and that they make many errors in communicating to mortals, but at the same time I assure you that nothing can be purer than a spirit friendship. I know that many come in who are not capable of advising, and yet who are so over anxious to control and talk that they make confusion in place of doing good.

The revolution which is to come will be seen as only now fairly begun. I know of nothing better than to wait and yet work on. I see you moving on with strength of faith which will carry you safely through every emergency into a haven of rest with those who are never weary of waiting, never tired of communion with their earth friends.

I am glad to see that a stronger, better class of spirits have taken control of spiritual matters, and I do assure you that all will change just as soon as their influence reaches high places. I would, as ever, encourage and be your friend.

R. B. M.

Good morning, my dear husband. This is a beautiful morning for us to write, so bright, clear and electric. We have only to come in your sphere of thought and spirit, when at once the flow of magnetism begins, and we are able to impart something of our life to you. At first our influence comes imperfectly, and then it is followed up with strength, dependent on the state of the atmosphere and yourselves from whom we gather, according to our needs. In fact, my dear husband, the effort which we make to communicate with our friends can scarcely be understood or appreciated by them. You saw how long it took me in that visit to Moravia to gather sufficient power to express myself then when so much was at hand to aid me. All that is spiritual and direct will of necessity be fragmentary and irregular, so to speak, not so much on our account as from the fact that we are obliged to use material senses and forms to express ourselves. The greatest difficulty sometimes occurs when one would expect the most from us. If we enter your homes and find you passive and impressible, we can bring to the mental faculties beautiful evidence of our presence. The majority, however, are not satisfied with this, and in most cases become positive at the very moment that we have prepared the most powerful manifestation.

F. is a beautiful medium, but there is little use trying to convince her of her power, from the fact that she requires constant tests, and places herself in such a position toward us that our influence is immediately thrown off. The very antagonism which at times she feels arises from the fact that spirits are making her resist us. I do not grieve relative to her in this direction. I know that she will gain here all that her inner desires long for while in the body. G. is gaining strength, and will not, I think, suffer again from the darker shadows which took such strong hold upon her will. B. needs a change from present scenes. You need not feel uneasy about them; we will help to direct and guide them. E. is the same peaceful, loving spirit I have ever seen her. She is constantly impressed in her life-work, and will be adequate to all its changes. I have many loving spirits beside our children to assist me. They are all faithful to you, and will bring you to see how perfect and divine is the guidance of angels.

     Your faithful wife, FANNY.

MY DEAR LOVING FATHER—Your circle journeys with you, and at every place, when you give us opportunity, we speak to your spirit through others. Meanwhile we journey with you side by side imparting our strength, while in turn you aid us to move higher in this beautiful domain of thought, wherein we find all that the soul requires for its growth and development. I am always telling you of the beautiful home in which we dwell—always speaking to your spirit of the harmony which flows between our lives and yours, and yet I do not half convey to you an idea of the glory which surrounds us here. We rejoice to see the rapidity with which our philosophy moves onward in the earth and over it everywhere, speaking to the soul with the voice of peace and love, silent to many, and yet to thousands loud-spoken. Oh, my dear father, what would heaven and the life immortal be without the sweet intercourse of love? Do not feel uneasy about the winter; we will be with you wherever you are, and the way will be peaceful. You will stay at home nearly all the time. I see that G. is improving all the time. B.

is a little uneasy without any cause. We think sometimes, however, that we cannot blame him. F. is the same unbeliever. Well, never mind, we can bear it, if she can, and will make her surprise greater when she joins us here. E. holds converse with us at all times. *Mary* is with me to-day, and all the dear ones join to bless you, with your loving circle. ANNA.

MY DEAR BROTHER—I speak in my own way to you, and I do hold communion with you in and through our own thoughts, which speak more than manifestations in and through other means expressed. I do not object to spirit communion, nor do I fear its influence as I did when in earth-life. I then shrank from it, because of the many strange things connected with it. To me these exist no longer, and I am happy in pursuing it in my own way. I do impress F., and she does accept many impressions from me. I am glad to be able to tell you that I am quietly pressing *my own* development in my own way. More, soon, to you. AGATHA.

MY DEAR FRIEND—I come in behalf of the many mediums who look to you as their vindicator, thanking you with grateful feelings for having so nobly taken their part and making their cause, as it were, thine own. There is still more to be done; and now that the influence of fear seems to be settling away before the strong steady tide of truth, we shall be glad to join and assist you to set forth still other evidence why mediums should not be held responsible for that which is called error. The earlier *cry of "humbug"* gave place to that of *"electricity,"* while but few seemed to have enough common sense to perceive how great a stride in the direction of truth had been made, the former cry meaning *nothing*, whilst the later in fact means *everything*. So great and comprehensive is the term *electricity*, though so thoughtlessly used, that those to whom we looked for its definition seemed least of all able to answer. If spirit intercourse, including the lively manifestations that are made, is mere *"humbug,"* or *nothing*, then it is idle to talk about it, as *nothing* from *nothing* leaves *nothing* as the remainder. Unfortunately, however, or otherwise, with electricity there is always *something* to create, *something* to use, and *something* left, when all and every known thing else is exhausted.

But touching that word "conditions" which mediums so naturally and generally fall back upon, why not honestly and carefully take it up and help them to arrange and watch results. Begin with each *so-called* medium, according to his or her peculiar phase of prophecy or spiritual gift, and honestly determine what of it is *"humbug"* or *nothing*, and what of it is *"electricity"* or *something*. See if your common sense will not enable you to rise superior to the outside pressure of *somebody's* dogmatic authority who seems never to have stopped to think and determine what Paul meant when he said, *"there is a natural body and there is a spiritual body!"* Was Paul a fool, think you, when he told the philosophers and *savans* of his day, *that concerning spiritual gifts he would not have them ignorant?* We tell you, friend, that the meanest spiritual gift is worth development — worth somebody's care, no matter who may cry "humbug."

If a small pan of burning charcoal is placed in a close room with living human beings, they droop and die, because of the primates of the life atmosphere being overcome or exhausted by the burning coals! Can anybody see the process by which this is done with the natural eye? Alas for *ignorance* and fear of the *ignorant*, how many beautiful instruments of the angels are forced out of their proper spheres and made to pervert every higher faculty of the spirit, because they ask for something beyond the narrow comprehension of men whose limited experience makes them but little superior to parrots and monkeys;

When men and women mediums acquire the noble independence and courage that will not only harmonize themselves but others who come into their presence also, then will begin the dawn of a new era of more independent manifestations of spirit power. Nor is the day distant when those two dreadful words, *respectable* and *scientific*, will shake hands in the simplicity of a true manhood, in which will be recognized the glory of nature and the beauty of truth. *Life* and *Love* are active, and the unwearied efforts of angels (among whom are your kindred friends) are making conditions old and grand as nature, and which are certain to be understood and conformed to by man, when he sees in himself that the only barriers to progress are his own cowardly fears. Write, my friend, and be as ever the friend and champion of such as was your friend,

ACHSA SPRAGUE,
with ROSA AMEDEY.

MY DEAR HUSBAND—I am very glad to meet you, and I have purposely drawn you here again where I can bring to you the fresh garlands we have gathered to inspire you with courage and mark out the way of truth and life. We know that your faith is straight, and that the light is unfailing and always the same and certain. In your spirit there is a fullness of faith which cannot fail to make you content under whatsoever circumstances of life you may be placed. There are many changes before you, and I want you to be strong to bear them, for they will bring you joy and gladness. The spirit circles which have more especial charge of the things of earth, were never stronger than now, and the time has come when the many prophecies which they have been so long speaking of will certainly be unfolded. Be open to the impressions which come, and quietly act them out without fear.

I see the dear ones at home, and have nothing to ask in regard to them. F. cannot help her unbelief; it is a condition which she inherits, and she is positive against all that she does not understand, particularly when there is the slightest danger of its striking at the foundation of that which she regards as truth. She will not accept it as you do until she comes to this side, where all the beautiful realities of life immortal stand face to face with her. All F.'s affections, intuitions and inspirations, have a material foundation. This to her is just; hence we can forgive all opposition and unbelief, for we know that she is sincere. G. is better; I have great hope of her, and must think, if she is kept along quiet and peaceful, that she will overcome her malady. I want that she should live out her natural life on earth, as I know it will be better for her. Do not wonder if E. becomes a little disquieted; she has a constant draft upon her. I am always glad when I see them making ready to take a journey, for it is the best thing for her to do. B. is doing well—dear child. His disposition is so harmonious and perfect that you will have no greater happiness than being with him. The conditions of his life were more perfect, and we understood each other better, when he came to us. Then my spirit influence was so directed to him and there concentrated that he is indeed beautiful. I wanted to have him just as he is, and I am satisfied. So are you, at least I trust you are, as your spirit tells me so.

I am writing such a long letter to you, while here stand many of your friends waiting to talk with you. Anna is here, also Mary, Agatha, and all the loving ones, with your own dear wife,

FANNY.

MY DEAR OLD FRIEND—How glad I am of this opportunity to speak with you, and tell you of the glory which surrounds the believer who not only thinks but acts his faith in all things. You are going to be carried on with a degree of power which will show you how constantly we have cared for you. I am not telling you strange tales to please and encourage you only, but I will help you in many ways to lift the veil and look beyond the shadows of the present into the clearer days when justice and equity will be known as the foundation of all governments, and man will be in himself an individual capable of dispensing justice, from the fact that he has angel guides and teachers who make him to be the worthy temple of truth. There is not one of the many spirits of both ancient and modern times with whom you and I spoke, and recorded their communications in a book,* but what has to a greater or lesser extent become your friend. Work on in your way, for in it is proof of individuality. Your usefulness will live after you, and generations will bless your memory.

I am your friend, JOHN GRINNELL.

Father, dear, we are so glad to be with you in the realities of affection and love. You are not to be left alone, nor will the changes that are taking place about you remove the foundation which our friends have helped to lay for you. Keep good heart, and do not fear to act and speak as you are impressed, for you know not how strong and perfect the influence is with you ofttimes. Be sure of our love, and as ever live in truth and affection with your own loving ones,

ANNA, MARY, ISABELLA, ELIZABETH.

MY FRIEND—As you have taken up the line of march with us, and frequently given utterance to our impressions in defence of mediums, we find in you our medium for circulating truth. I see but few that have the courage to speak out as you do.

The world to-day, through its great representatives, presents a singular compound. While the public is not willing to take the word of a Spiritualist, the nation seems quite ready and will-

* Ordeal of Life, published by Colby & Rich, Boston.

ing to present and accept oaths of office as sure guarantees, and thus the most sacred of trusts is placed in the keeping of men whose word, as it is proven, is as valueless as the wind. I know that it makes a great difference with the world as it goes, for the reason that all religious subjects or matters are left apart from the things of business or every-day life. If the so-called great minds of your nation to-day are called upon to hold converse on religious subjects, they will tell you that the Sabbath is the day set apart for such business. This idea has so long prevailed that it is no wonder, nor do the spirits marvel at the fact that there is no longer either religion or philosophy in the church.

Spiritualists as a body are regarded as deluded and unsafe in council—are not expected to speak the truth—cannot be placed on committees when all things under investigation are before the face and eyes of those who are called to witness and examine them! They are deluded who dare to say that they cannot believe the incomprehensible things which theology teaches because they do not understand them! Thus showing that the whole basis of what is called "truth as it is in Christ Jesus" is not to be regarded as reliable, from the fact that no man or mind can explain or make plain what for instance is called the trinity, only by the acceptation of a mystery which no human reason can grasp or settle. And yet the unreasoning man who accepts this incomprehensible mystery in the sense conferred on it by a religious sect or a dogmatic priest, is held to be not only a respectable but a trustworthy citizen, and in short is regarded as a man of sound mind and principles, whilst he who has the moral courage to say that he does not believe the mystery which he cannot unravel by any mental process or power of reasoning, is deemed to be *deluded*, and as I have before said, is held to be unworthy of belief on any subject for that very cause. In all or most instances those who have seceded from an old dogma have held to the rotten plank on which they floated away, and too often through what is called *reverence* have builded their new structure on the one idea or *plank* which they still hold to and revere.

When a wanderer comes out of the old house who has nothing left, it is difficult to find a place to worship or to rest in. Spiritualism is the only truth that admits of a complete gathering together of men and women who can agree to disagree, and draw about them that higher power and influence which in disagreement still keeps steadily going forward and increasing more rapidly than any sect, society or organization ever started in this century.

Its first and most important lesson is to individualize and make men separately and entirely responsible for their own lives and conduct. We have worked to reveal man to himself and to show him his own capabilities by removing from him the fear of death and hell.

Alas, that the fear of death should make man a liar and a coward! In the days when old Rome stood before the nations of the world as the grand climax of all that was great and glorious, her most sublime heroes and philosophers were those who faced, nay, courted death for that which seemed to them honor and glory; and yet not *one* of those loftier souls were deemed to be deluded, *unreliable fools!*

They who read and reflect cannot fail to trace and perceive the certain intelligence of the invisible spiritual hosts which surrounded Socrates to the last moment of his earth-life! Was he indeed deluded? Would his word have been taken? Would he have been appointed to fill a place of trust? Alas, my friend, the strange incongruities which the leading religious minds of the world in all ages have held to be God's truth, are rapidly wearing away. The schoolhouse, the railway and the telegraph, have proved to be a comprehensible trinity which is leading man to know, first of *all*, himself; and thus becoming better acquainted with his fellow-man, and through that link upgoing nearer to God. When all else has been said, the last grand argument resorted to by the enemies of Spiritualism is the conduct of the mediums, the unreliability of their communications, and the subject-matter conveyed being so unlikely to come from that world where theology places God and his holy angels. If all the mediums who are known to yourself were to-day to stand side by side with the clergy, we would believe the former on their word before an angel tribunal rather than the latter, and credit a large balance in favor of the honesty of the mediums. ONE OF YOUR GUIDES.

MY DEAR HUSBAND—I am here to greet you and tell you the truths again which we have spoken so many, many times. We live in the glory of a life which is filled with light, and we look through all to see more plainly the lives of those to whom we are attracted and bound by the ties of consanguinity and spirits. You and I have learned in that light and life more of each other, more of ourselves, than we could have gained by a longer life on earth. I realize this every day as I advance and grow stronger in the faith which has made us more fully one. I know that you will love me more and more, and I fully realize how perfect the purpose of my death and all else that has occurred since. I have our family with us, and our home is more complete in the beauties which our united lives can create. Be sure that our children each and all have an individual life, and that ourselves are harmoniously blended in them. We will help to act the truths which our spirits so firmly hold, and we will live together ever and ever the same. I see that all is well. FANNY.

MY DEAR, BLESSED FATHER—You are welcome to our spirits everywhere that we can come to bless you. We do walk beside you and move away the shadows which fall in your pathway. Beautiful indeed is your home here. When you have sat down in conclave thus with us, I return to our home and add another picture to our walls. I show you as a traveler walking heavenward; I show you gathering the flowerets by the wayside and giving out from the abundance which we bring the light which is yet to brighten many a dark shadow and lighten many a burden. I paint the pictures and leave them here, so that you can see them when you come, and enjoy again the pleasures which life created out of the spiritual power which was with you when you knew it not. Oh, my dear father, it is a beautiful truth to know and fully appreciate all these connecting links with the loved ones on every side. Life can have no shadows when all is known to be divine wisdom and love. Be sure we are faithful ever to all. Your child, ANNA.

MY DEAR FRIEND—I am glad to meet you here for a brief season, and I fully realize the importance of using the time to the best advantage. I see that you are surrounded by many who love you, and it is indeed a joy to me to witness with what affection they cling to you. Do not think they would draw you from earth's duties; on the contrary, they speak to you with that courage which makes you meet all life's emergencies with content and peace. You know these are blessings, and I need not repeat them to you. I come to you as an old friend who would speak to you of matters just as I see them. First, all things are steadily advancing, and the basis is being made for a more wholesome action than the past has shown, and there will be a gradual rising into better results than have heretofore existed. A more intelligent class of men are being brought forward, and the past has been an education so positive that it will not be forgotten nor unheeded. We know that the time has been slow, and we look upon all the changes which have passed as just and needful. You will wait upon events which are to follow as orderly as the seasons. I know that you realize the wisdom of waiting, and I ask you to be patient; meanwhile the way will be plain to you to do all you were promised and to realize all that you were told. I see that all commercial and legitimate business will lead in the reform so certain to follow. R. B. M.

Yes, friend, I am here, and I am glad to be where you have so often found the spirit circles ready to greet you. I have introduced myself to your medium, and am happy to say that I feel quite at home. You are getting a start, now—I mean the Spiritualists. There are some strong shoulders to the wheel, and a fresh impetus seems given which they certainly deserve. I am glad to welcome all and every atom belonging to the truth, and I rejoice in being able to add my own testimony in the cloud of witnesses which surround you on every side. W. C.

MY DEAR SON—Thy father is with thee, and thy mother, and while the tide of spiritual things flows about thee I want thee to understand that no stronger link binds thee than the love which comes from thy father and mother, grandfather, and the circle of home.

Yes, dear father, I am here to answer your desires, and to make you feel that we can and will help you. I see that our home is brighter to-day, for we can gather near to you and make you to see almost as plainly into the angel-world as we do. Father, dear, our blessed mother is here with us. She tells me to say to you that you do not know how much we can and do do for you. In love, ever your own MARY.

Thomas, my dear brother, we are so happy to join thee, and at all times to extend to thee evidence of the affection of love which has never been removed from thee in the changes and struggles which have been like so much schooling to thy spirit, carrying thee forward and making thee to realize that thine inheritance hath been and is one that will not only bring thee into the kingdom of peace, but help others to come there as well. I have tried many times to manifest in thy home, and have made direct appeals to F., who invariably repels me, and I cannot do more than enjoy the truth which she possesses. I have seen her and spoken to her face to face, and yet she does not like to own my presence. I want to be understood as helping them, whereby I also help myself, as I have had a long struggle to convince myself that this is truth. Be sure, however, that I will speak to thee, and I know that thy spirit will answer me. I am often in the circle with thy children, and have been taught by them. I thank thee for thy love and patient faith, and as ever will come in the life of my spirit immortal to cheer and be cheered. In love,

ELIZABETH.*

MY DEAR HUSBAND—We gather wherever you give us an opportunity to speak love and progress to you. So strong have I grown that I feel now that we are both individuals, and yet one in spirit. I realize that death has not separated us, but on the contrary it has made us to understand each other far better than we should had we lived on until the present time in the earth-life. I have builded our house here out of the rich material you have provided me with, and you have nobly worked on to carry forward the good harvest of truth. How often, when we sit down together in the beautiful home, I wish you could be with

---

*The compiler has two grandmothers and several relatives and friends in the other life of this name, but no sister to his knowledge.

us, and I look away into the distance and see your spirit beckoning me to come to you. I go and answer your thought while I make your feet to tread along life's pathway with renewed vigor, always refreshed by my power and gladdened with my presence.

Lloyd is with me to-day. He is a wonderful spirit, and so full of vital power that he could carry you onward and forward to prosperity and peace.

Yes, ask me questions, if you like.

ANSWER TO QUERY—Our houses here will be united, and I can and do help to build and furnish it with and through your actions. Your house corresponds to your deeds, and will be builded by them.

That *Elizabeth* who just wrote is a friend of mine by the name of *Bush*, who is attached to our home, and is there in the house a great deal. She is very like F., and will continue to learn of you, and at times attempt control. She is gentle and peaceful, and is every way desirable as a friend. There are so many here who are anxious to communicate to you, that I half expect it is better that you should hear from me entirely. The girls are here, and our dear boys grown into maturity. You will know them when you come, for they are like us both. I sometimes think that my love goes out stronger to the dear boy living in earth-life than to all the rest. (*Elizabeth Bush* calls me sister *Fanny*, and I told her she might call you brother.) Oh, what a beautiful truth, and how perfect is the law that controls spirit, in or out of the body. I must say to you again that all are dear to me, and as ever I must repeat that I am your devoted and loving wife,

FANNY.

MY DEAR FRIEND—I am with you to-day full of hope and faith, and yet not without regrets. When I overlook the present state of the country, it is sad to see such an—I had almost said entire absence of honesty in and with business

men. On all sides, from the government officers down, men seek political influence for individual favors and patriotism, and the general good has ceased to have a claim upon those who occupy high places. Foreign influence and favoritism is rapidly undermining the nation, while the surface is glossed over with *words, words,* which have no meaning. I am not going to show a dark picture, for I am fully aware of this fact, namely, that it is needful to the future to be just where we are. Honest men will finally be brought out, better ways will be opened, and a revolution will follow in time to avert greater danger. Hence I can say to you fear not, and know me as ever your friend, ROBERT B. MINTURN.
Sept. 24th, 1873.

MY DEAR HUSBAND—We did not keep you waiting this morning. You told the medium that you would be here, and we came before you to make certain that nothing should come in before us to disturb the conditions which we required to offer you all our beautiful power. I know that you are happier when you feel that we are to meet you, and it matters not what the pleasures of the hour may be, nothing is beautiful and peaceful without us, and while we mingle silent and passive in all that you do, we still hold your spirit in the fond embrace of affection and love. I was with you in your journey and looked upon your meetings in different places, and we all try to make ourselves known to you in some way. I find you at this moment surrounded by a class of spirits who are anxious to give out through you some evidence of their presence, each intent upon the particular purpose in view with all their theories and thoughts, ready to convey as much or as little perhaps as they have learned in the spirit-world. I see that a number have gathered to impress your mind with a variety of subjects, all calculated to give the world something beyond the narrow limits of sectarian authority. I shall be most happy to see you able to give out all that will be given you, and I desire that you should also know that your whole family circle, including brother Rowland and all the rest who gather with you, are bringing their aid to have you outwork the particular result which is before you as one *kind* of medium. There is no such thing as idleness in any age or period of life, and as you have gathered in your harvest years so many wonderful truths, we shall still continue with you to make the fruits of that harvest more abundant, and thus give to you a four-fold reward. Be sure of the guiding care of those to whom we look for wisdom, and do not falter in the way of truth. You have gone through the worst. Those who smiled at your delusion begin to feel the strength of that tide which is moving forward and onward in divine order, entering hearts and houses, creating a joy and peace which will rise superior to every condition of the earth teachings. B. is at home to-day ; the sun shines softer there, and the old home looks cheery to us, notwithstanding so many changes have swept over it. G. is better, and from all I see is happier in being alone. F. is enjoying the new scenes before her in her travels, and E. is as ever the quiet, faithful wife. I am well pleased with all efforts for your health and happiness. I know all that this life of earth requires, and I can see you coming forward through all to the higher truths which belong to the spirit. There are many mistakes made in the earth-form, and too much power given to that which man calls authority, not only in theology but in all else. I am out of all of it now, and I want to see you live the life of freedom and peace. In that you and I will journey together. I shall help you in the affections, and will not be selfish in one single thought or feeling. I am going to protect you, and you know that in your family circle all will come to bless and cheer you with your own loving FANNY.

Talk to me, my brother. I come to-day full of the spirit of love and truth to begin anew the communication between us, and as far as possible to aid you in undertaking the life which is yet before you. I see so much to engross thought and attract attention that it is difficult to say what is the most important. Your nation is passing through a strange struggle, one which all the wisdom of the land can scarcely meet and cope with. Selfish men have so long stood in the way of truth, that naught remains but to cope with and have the struggle over. How it is to be done to prevent a monarchy, is the question which is agitating the spheres at this time. There are few, comparatively, very few who understand the danger, and I may say still fewer who are capable of giving the counsel and advice which the case requires. I look upon the united forces drawn up under the guidance of spirits who are still interested in the affairs of earth, and I hear their words of counsel. I feel to assure you that some strange revolutions and wonderful changes are to take place in our nation before we shall see a better order of things. I know that all classes of society, every department of life, is reaching out to the angel-world for counsel and aid. I realize how constantly, on the other hand, the spirit-world is seeking proper mediums through whom to act in the best and wisest way. You must be wise, and look for help from the right source. It will be granted you, and you will enjoy to the fullest all that your faith has promised. I see how directly the spirit-world will bring its power, and how completely it will secure to humanity that measure of wisdom and guidance which the present generation can and will secure and adapt. Do not think that we forget you, nor doubt the interest we have in you. I want you to hold communion with us in thought, and I know you will be saved many of the sorrows which fall upon those who have put their trust in the fleeting things of the material world. Faithful ever, ROWLAND.

Jan. 21*st*, 1875.

My Dear One—We came in with you, and did not mean that you should go until we had brought our offerings of love and peace to you. We know how your heart reaches out to us, and how tame and dull life would become without our presence and care, and we love to linger to scatter the clouds which fall on life's pathway. We feel great pleasure in seeing your faith strengthen under all circumstances, so that you can look away into our life and feel that you are journeying *home.* We do not ask that all life's duties should be light, nor that you should have no cares, for we would not remove you from the field of effort which makes you to draw nearer to us. Beautiful indeed are the scenes which open to us here, where so many have gathered to bring to the affections all the joys which were theirs in life to know and live.

They who greet you at different places where you go, are only a small number compared to the many who are with you as so many acquaintances, sometimes learning from you, and then again giving to you the strength which you need to give to those who look to you for care, counsel and advice. I am glad to see our dear ones at home. The angels come close to guard them there, and the holy benediction of my love falls upon them like the dew of affection, serene and sweet.

Do not think that I forget you. Wherever you are my spirit can go and bring to you thoughts which seem strange, and yet which, if understood, would be found linked with some friend long ago known and perhaps loved. Many come and try to impress you, and many others would be glad to write and communicate save that they know not how to control a medium's hand. I have taught many how to reach the loving ones who have watched and waited for their coming, and find much pleasure in so doing. In fact, it is a part of my life-business in the spirit-home. I see that E. is talking of returning. Her health is improved, and she will be stronger in her development of the spiritual. F. accepts impres-

sions under another name. G. is almost constantly guarded by her spirit sisters, whose care it is to keep out all inharmonious influences. We have no difficulty in coming at home. The house is so full of our presence that we seem to live there with you, my dear one. I must not be selfish when there are so many here to greet you with their love. I am so happy in our meetings now that we understand each other as never before. Then, so many of my friends are constantly coming in to make the cloud of witnesses more complete. Accept my love in the same great abundance to all, with the assurance of my watchful care and devotion. Your own
FANNY.

www.ingramcontent.com/pod-product-compliance
Lightning Source LLC
Chambersburg PA
CBHW020730100426
42735CB00038B/1850